SMART BRAIN RIGHT BRAIN

Learn to Colour

Om KIDZ
An imprint of Om Books International

First Published in 2021 by

Om Kidz | Om Books International

Corporate & Editorial Office
A-12, Sector 64, Noida 201 301
Uttar Pradesh, India
Phone: +91 120 477 4100
Email: editorial@ombooks.com
Website: www.ombooksinternational.com

Sales Office
107, Ansari Road, Darya Ganj
New Delhi 110 002, India
Phone: +91 11 4000 9000
Email: sales@ombooks.com

Author: Swayam Ganguly
Editor: Nandita Bhardwaj
Art & Design: Anshuman Pandey, Gaurav Bhandari, Harish Arya

ISBN: 978-93-5276-849-3

Printed in India

10 9 8 7 6 5 4 3 2 1

CONTENTS

1. An Introduction to Colouring

Do you like the colour Blue?
Do you like Green instead?
Or is your favourite colour Red?
With so many colours to choose,
Get a colouring book to use.
Colouring is smart, colouring is fun.
Colour the blue sky and the yellow sun.
It's time to colour! You'll be fine.
Don't be afraid to go outside the lines.

Colour is everywhere! Look around you. How many colours do you see? Can you even imagine a world without the colourful flowers, trees, birds, animals and the bright clothes your mama brings? Colours are an important part of our lives. Each and everything in our world has its own colour. Wouldn't it be so boring without colours?

Colouring is so much fun! The best part about colouring is that you can do it alone as well as with friends and family.

DID YOU KNOW?

The first colour that a baby sees is **RED**.

2. What Do You Need?

Colouring books and colouring supplies

There are many colouring books available that you can choose from, with many interesting topics like transport, space, animals, words, cartoons, numbers, fruits and vegetables. Have fun as you learn.

To colour, you need supplies. You can choose from crayons, water colours and paints that come in so many different and attractive colours.

Finger painting is when you use your fingers to paint instead of using crayons, colour pencils or brushes. It's a whole lot of fun and also helps you colour naturally and easily.

The right colouring grip

It is very important to hold your crayon or colour pencil in the right way while colouring.

DID YOU KNOW? The prehistoric cavemen were the first painters and they used their fingers to colour their art.

Hold the small ones near the tip and long ones away from the tip.

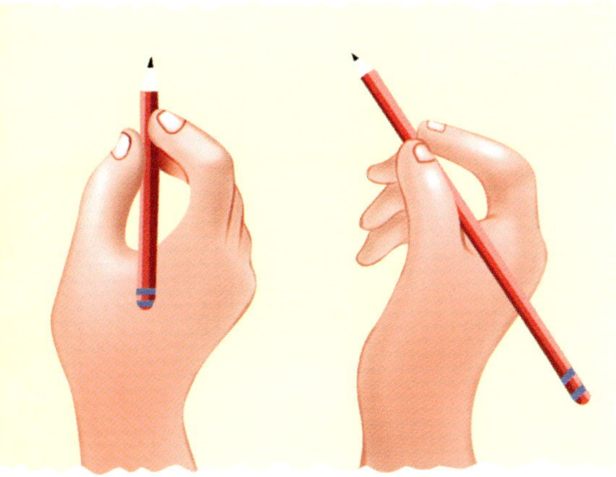

Right way to hold a pencil

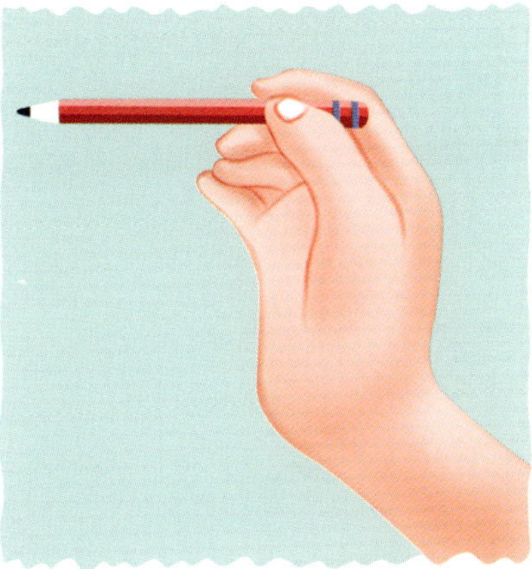

Wrong way to hold a pencil

To colour, you can also use paint brushes that are thin or thick, depending on their use. Hold the brush like you would hold a pencil.

3. Primary Colours

There are three types of colours: Primary, Secondary and Tertiary.

Primary Colours

Red, blue and yellow are the three **Primary Colours**.

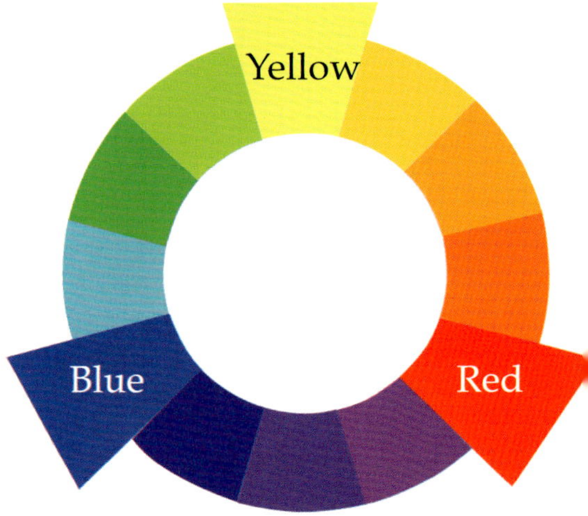

The colour of an apple or a rose is red. The sky and the ocean are blue in colour. A banana and a sunflower are yellow in colour.

Activity

Look at the three objects given below. Can you identify the objects first and then use the three primary colours to colour these objects?

DID YOU KNOW?

The sun is yellow but from space it looks white.

4. Secondary Colours

When we mix two primary colours, we get **Secondary Colours**. For example, when we mix red and blue, we get purple. If we mix blue and yellow, we get green. Red and yellow will give orange.

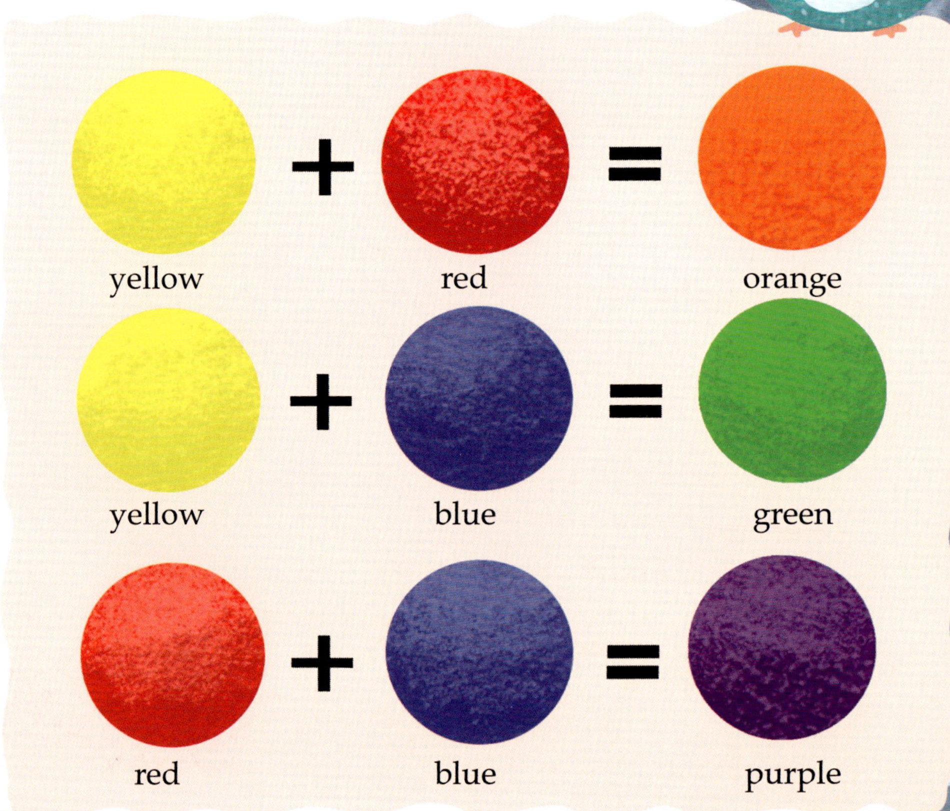

Activity

1. Look at the colour combinations. Can you identify which colours will be formed when the two colours are mixed with each other?

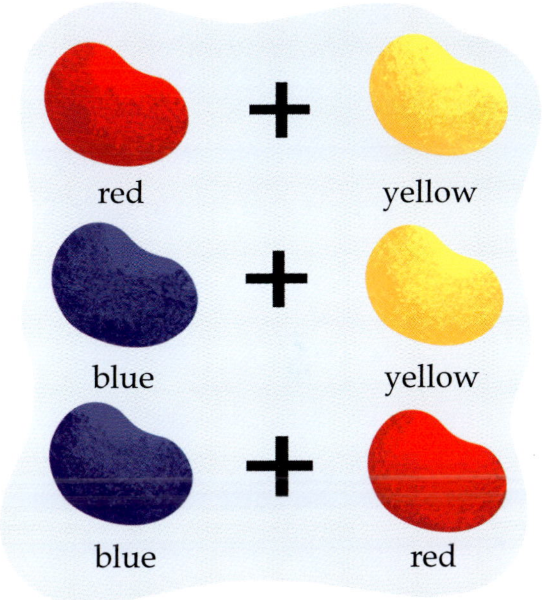

2. Below are the images of an orange, a leaf and an aubergine. Can you identify each one and colour them in the right colour?

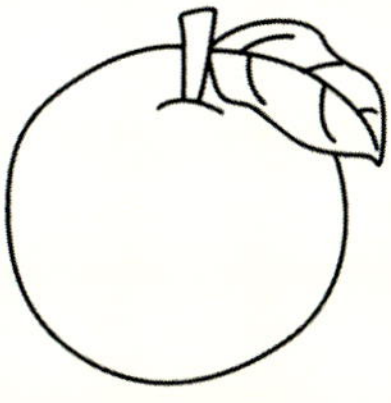

POCKET FACT

When light shines on an object, some colours bounce off the object and others are absorbed by it. Our eyes only see the colours that are bounced off or reflected.

5. Tertiary Colours

When we mix equal parts of both primary and secondary colours, we get **Tertiary Colours**. There are six tertiary colours: red-orange, yellow-orange, yellow-green, blue-green, blue-purple, and red-purple.

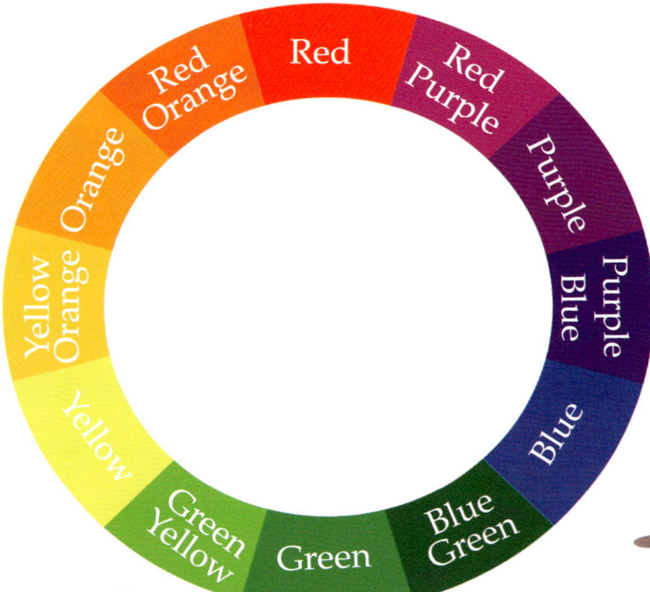

POCKET FACT

The three primary colours, red, blue, and yellow, are the only colours that cannot be made by mixing other colours.

Let's mix colours and practise by colouring the butterflies with the right combination of colours.

6. Rainbow of Colours

Have you ever seen a rainbow? Sometimes, when the sun is shining on one side, but it is raining too, you can see a rainbow form in the sky. It is shaped like an arc that has seven colours, namely, violet, indigo, blue, green, yellow, orange and red, also called VIBGYOR for short.

DID YOU KNOW?

The rainbow is formed by the light from the sun being broken up by water droplets. The sun's light is 'white', but the water droplets break it up into seven different colours, always in this order—red, orange, yellow, green, blue, indigo, violet.

How to colour a rainbow?

Take a large sheet of white paper. Using a black crayon, draw seven arches or half-circles that curve towards the clouds and trees on the top of the paper and end on the bottom of the page. After that, add the sky and ground to the painting. Start with completing and colouring the drawing below:

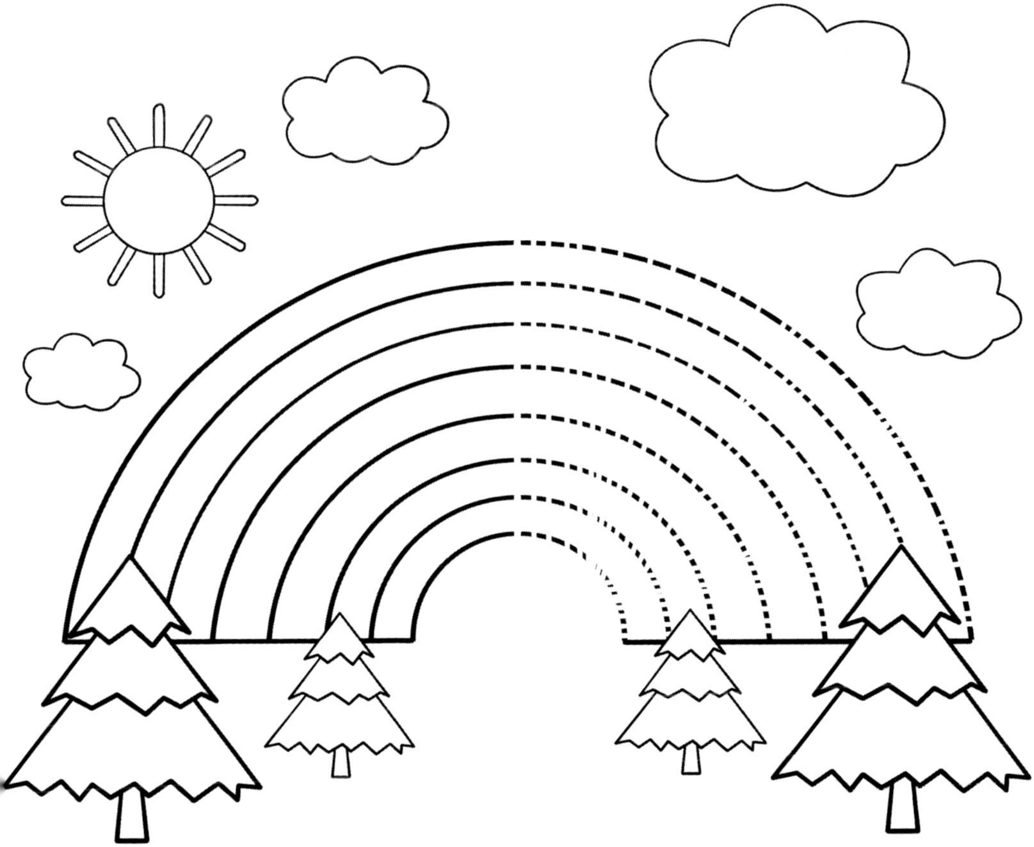

7. Colour Wheel

The Colour Wheel shows us the primary, secondary and tertiary colours and how these colours are related to each other. The Colour Wheel is also used to organise colours and reminds artists how to mix and think about colours. So, it will be very helpful for you while colouring.

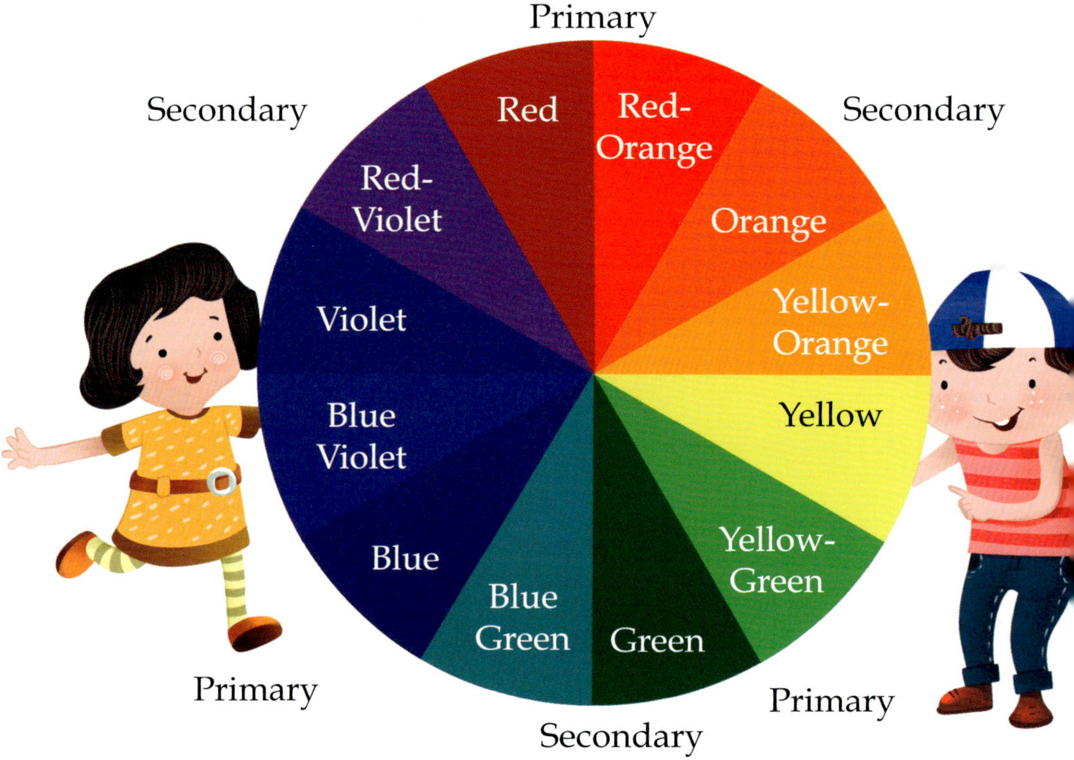

Primary Colours cannot be made from other colours. Artists create all the other colours of the rainbow by mixing together the primary colours.

Secondary colours are made by mixing two primary colours. Each secondary colour is made from the two primary colours closest to it on the colour wheel. Red-orange, yellow-orange, yellow-green, blue-green, blue-violet, and red-violet are the tertiary colours and we get them by mixing equal parts of primary and secondary colours.

Activity

Here's a fun activity to remember colours better. Take two printouts of the colour wheel and hang them in your room, one in colour and one in black and white. Use the colour printout to remind you of the colours in the colour wheel and use the black and white printout to test what you remember.

DID YOU KNOW?

Horses can only see two colours. Cats and dogs also do not see as many colours as we do. They see only shades of blue and yellow.

8. Using Black and White Colours

Be careful while using white and black colours to make your painting lighter or darker. Do not use too much of black and white as they dull your art and take away the life from all the other colours. When we mix black and white, the colour grey is produced.

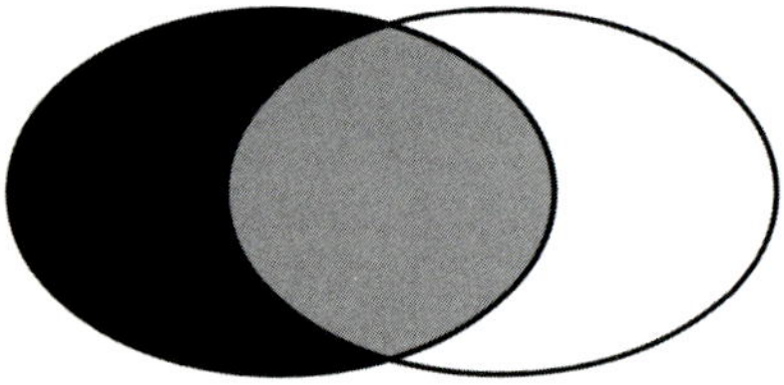

black + white = grey

Making colours lighter or darker

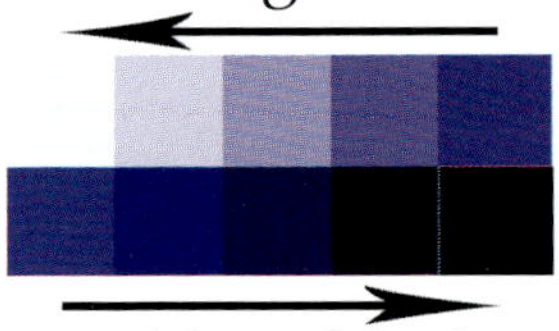

To make a colour lighter, add a small amount of white. The more white you add, the lighter a colour is. Remember that white lightens a colour but does not make it bright. For example, if we add white to red, we get pink.

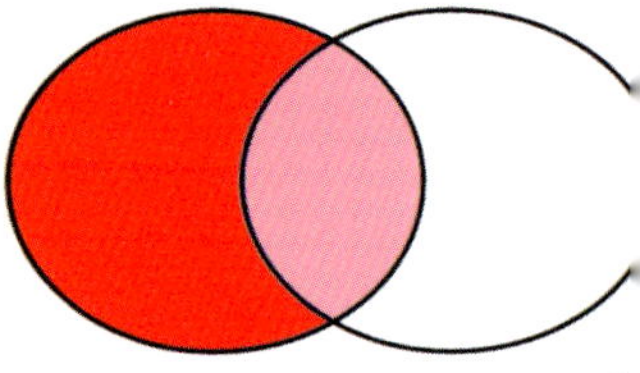

red + white = pink

To make a colour darker, add a small amount of black. If you add too much black, your colour will be almost black. For example, we get dark blue when we add black to blue and dark red when we add black to red.

Different quantities of the two colours will give you different shades when mixed

Adding white | Adding black | Adding grey

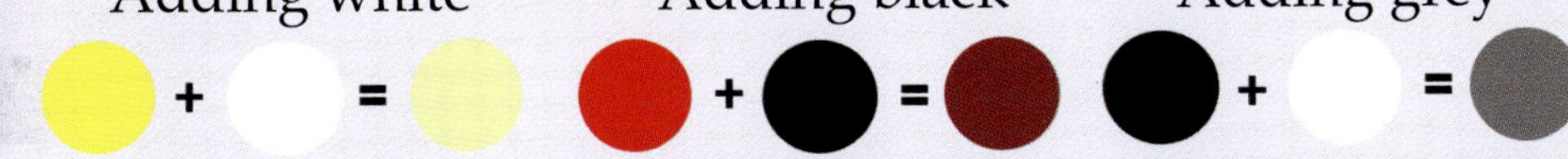

Adding white to a colour lightens it

Adding black to a colour darkens it

By mixing varying amounts of black and white you can get different shades of grey

9. Warm and Cool Colours

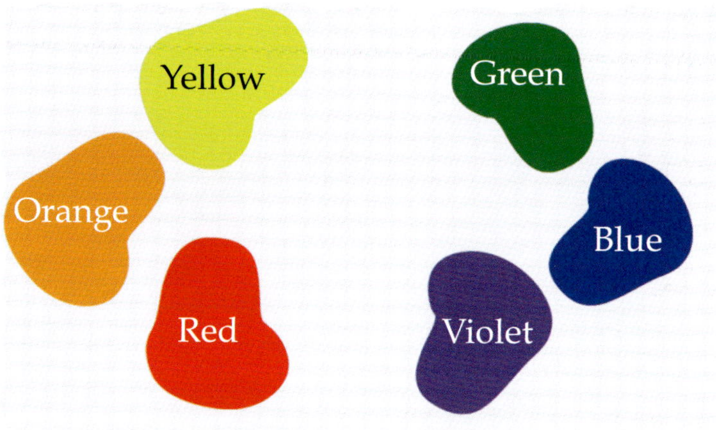

Warm colours are red, yellow and orange. These are colours that depict sunlight, heat and emotions like excitement, anger and frustration. Cool colours are blue, green and violet. The cool colours go with cold things like ice and feelings like sadness, comfort and calm.

Warm Colours

Cool Colours

POCKET FACT

We see warm colours more easily than cool colours.

However, a colour can be warm, as well as cool depending on its shade. Here are the cool and warm shades of the primary colours.

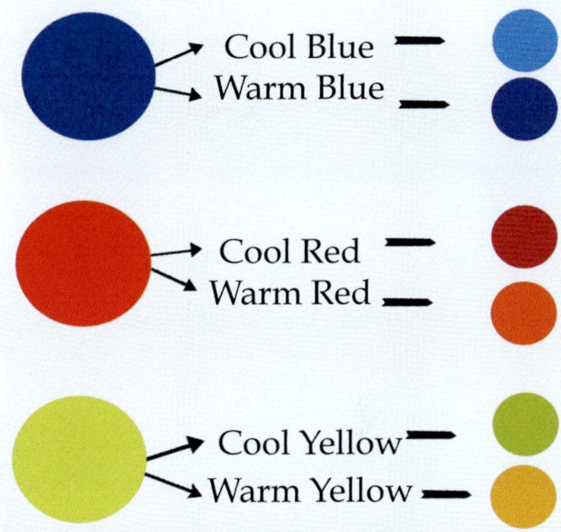

The sun is an example of an object with a warm colour while the moon has a cool colour.

DID YOU KNOW?

Warm colours make a room feel warm, while cool colours make a room feel cool. Warm colours make the room seem smaller because the walls feel closer while cool colours make the walls feel further away, which makes it feel larger.

10. Tips to Colour

- To make your colouring smoother, add 2-3 sheets of plain paper underneath the page that you are colouring. This will cushion your colouring and make it better.
- Keep your coloured pencils well sharpened.

Remember, sharper pencils make better colours!

- Don't put too much pressure with your pencil when you are colouring to make your colour dark.
- Colour in a circular motion for a smooth and nice finish.

• Colour in the same direction and colour from the outside and go to the inside to keep your work neat and tidy. Do not change direction suddenly while colouring, otherwise your work will look messy and untidy.

• While colouring, keep between the lines.
• Two tricks to help you stay within the lines:
  • Make a thick border on the shape that you are colouring. This will help you to not colour outside the lines.
  • You can also draw a glue outline on the borders and let it dry. This will create bumps on the borders and you will know when you are colouring outside the lines.

Colour within the lines

Practise colouring 'Ted the Turtle' to help you stay within the lines when you colour:

• Before you colour, choose what you want to colour and the crayons you want to use.

• Colour one section or part at a time.

• If you want an area to be light, use less pressure on your crayon while colouring. Use a bit more pressure if you want an area to be darker in colour. This is known as **shading**.

• Colour pictures that have big borders. This will help you colour more easily.

• Make colouring a part of your daily routine just as you brush your teeth daily.

Activity 1: Win the Race

Match the colours with the cars.

Let's play and have some fun with colours!

What you will need is:

- Paint
- Four toy cars (coloured red, blue, yellow and green)
- A large rectangular sheet of paper
- Masking tape (to hold the paper in place so that it does not move while you are painting)

What to do: Match the colours with the paint and toy cars for some super fun!

Let's play: Put a blob of paint on each end of the paper and mix up the paint blobs so that the cars need to cross each other's paths to match the colour. Try and roll the car on the coloured path made by the paint towards the finishing point of the race. For example, the blue car will race on the blue path. See which of your friends is able to drive the car on the right coloured path.

Activity 2: Identify and Colour

Identify the nursery rhyme and colour the following picture.

Identify the following fruits and colour them accordingly.

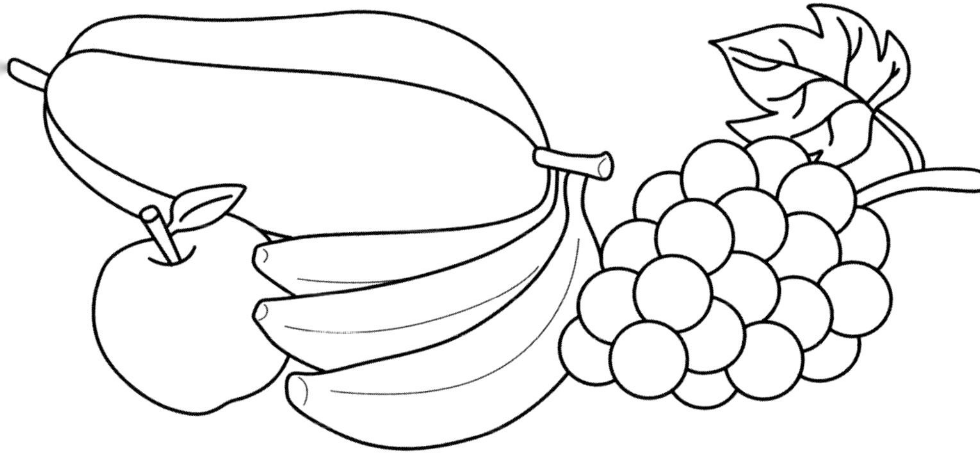

Activity 3: Farm Colour by Numbers:

Colour the picture and see if your choice of colours matches the answers.